John Ray, a 17th century British naturalist who strove to know the unknowable (everything about flora and fauna), said something that fits interestingly with Heim, who aims not so much to know what can't be known but to express as clearly and cleanly the greatest complexities. Ray says, "[S]he that uses many words for explaining any subject, doth, like the cuttlefish, hide himself for the most part in his own ink." Heim's statements, phrases, clauses, can be quite short, curt, making us leap distances in our thought process to get to the next one. But in using this direct route she allows us to travel far. And she reveals so much of herself, of her brilliance, by letting us find it for ourselves. Who would have anticipated, indeed, "what we are becoming—in constraint, in circumspection?"

Where one might predict a descent into floridity—poems about love or a baby—this poet finds a new angle. Tender, yes, but not soft. In fact, when she draws her bow at all we might hold dear, she aims for the bone instead of the flesh. To a baby, where one might normally say, "Shush—close your eyes. Everything will be all right," this poet says, "Persevere, little lamb. Only hunger is straight." And when missing someone beloved, she says, "Secrecy, obviously, is old." Tenderness is a tough bird, it seems. In "She Thinks That Is Which Appears to Be" there's a piercing passage:

> "The only cure for madness
> is forgetfulness,
> and in these few years she's seemed
> insane all the time."

But we are still within Heim's teleology of frank and uncompromising trajectories. That poems ends with the blunt and true monostich: "The head is just an organ for borrowing."

Oh, now I've devolved into listing a bunch of examples. That could go on, like the titular table, for miles, but to what purpose? There is no example of the poet's lovely choices and marvelous worldview that replaces the joy and heat of reading the book. Just read the book. I'll end this intro right where I started, and you start where this intro ends, if not sooner. You can read it in the dark; you don't even need a book light or a flashlight under your covers. It provides its own radiance. Heim's words illuminate each page. I don't know how to leave off talking about it, so I'll let her do it for me. Think about the mysterious but precise length of time we have—no more and no less, but as yet unknowable—in our bodies, in our worlds. Stefania Heim would say it like this: "This hotel, a wet night that extends."

TABLE OF CONTENTS

MISERICORDIA

Because of the hills, we feel
lonely, because the river smells

closer than it is.
The country is only one language.

We say comfort and mean
that though there are more stars here

than we can imagine,
there is still one small, cream room.

It is small enough.

This is one kind of writing:
At the base of every hill

I imagine there is water.
But the water is farther off.

TERMINI

1.
Today there's no one who doesn't look
like someone I miss. How can we know
what to ask for, what not to ask for?

Morning is belly-heavy, complicated
by roads. Your turtle shape departed,
I'm ridiculous in my state of undress.

2.
Out again alone
among the strict, old hedges.

It's murder
to get lost here but I'll try.

Delicate lattice at the base
of blank unbudging

and I'm wishing all the wishers
away.

3.
White sails cluttering
the horizon. Everything
bends. It is not strong

to not want. The sky is
kind and blue and hurts our eyes.
Where have we been

that we can still visit?
Past holiday, past Tuesday.
How do you feel?

Let us read our stars and
discredit them. Sit beside me
here. Write me letters.

Let us neither one go first.

FURIOUS WATER

Reason to believe the ships
will return. Want to.

We are getting out the
big sticks.

We are bracing
for the next kiss.

Sails across the face
of wind. Or leaning in to it.

Washed, sad, we are
otherwise inconstant.

Our wildly associative
self-serving way.

And what lengthens
in summer isn't nearly enough.

MOVING PICTURE

These friends nourish improbable ambitions. Summer ends and the rain pours down. While his sister embraces an older married gentleman, a religious procession trails gaudily through the town. If a wife runs away she always takes the baby with her. A desperate search to settle. What each admires is afar.

A LARGE MIRROR UNLOADED
FROM A TRUCK IN THE SUN

Participation relegated to sleeping near
the open window. My great failure

has always been not imagining the future
but in managing myself. Your thumbprint, please,

before we launch the new rhetoric. I know
when I grovel I am plain. I've actually had a dream

about this building, and it feels soon enough to me now.
For all the reasons we are short of breath, approximate.

Passion clusters as though circumstance. A terrible
child, I grow apart. According to the original

rules, burn everything. Who could have anticipated
what we are becoming—in constraint, in circumspection.

I'll think of some experiment to move us,
focusing on the lenses learned.

CONSIDERING THE LIMITATIONS
OF THE FORCE OF MY WILL

Knowing what I
want and wanting it.

Knowing what I
want and wanting not

to want it. Knowing what
wanting wants

of me, wants me to cease
wanting for what

I want to want
to come. To want

wanting to stop
its urgency. To be in want.

To feel its urgency.
Angry with the want,

with the thing
that is not, with the what

it represents. With the how
it is not

what it represents.
And how I do not,

can not, wanting,
know

the want of the thing
I want:

The what of it.

HEART PUMPING FOR TWO
PUMPS CAVERNOUSLY

There's a hidden body
in your painting! I was ready
to be fine again

until that white dog
bit me. Alone in the bed
I'm all-night dreaming

at the edge of a cliff.

This constant serving up
of retroactive inevitability. Soon,
of a group, I'll say:

One of those is mine. That one.
The pull and grieve of her
so far unimaginable.

MOVING PICTURE

We know immediately that she wants a child. She has been waiting just a little bit too long.

We can't see the train, shrieking bodily from its distance. Everyone else who matters hovers whisperingly off screen.

THE LOWEST POSSIBLE LIMIT
OF PERPETUAL SNOW

A buzzing
like something

living within.
We painted a found wood slab blue.

We used it as a table.

Tell me when crying becomes particular,
uncommon, an illumination

not otherwise planned.
The one who stays thinks of weather

as a catalog of lasts.
Regarding

comfort, another Sunday clacks along.

A trick of light:
two of me in a mirror,

and in the corner, you, who also knows.

Greetings from blank
where the sky has just opened up.

WE'RE SO HAPPY NOW,
THERE IS SO MUCH MORE
TO TALK ABOUT

Scars, everywhere, are irresistible:
I am a heterogeneous

thing, waiting for you
to come home.

Weeks hinge and fold over
themselves, longings crystallize

into patterns
of return. Tonight

is not a bridge,
nor is it scattered among many

other nights of great emulsion.
Secrecy, obviously, is old.

By morning, another
mountaintop,

where we are learning to fear
and then not fear

snow.

ONLY TWO PASSENGERS FACING
EACH OTHER AT OPPOSITE
SIDES OF THE CAR

Snow melting
torrential
on the
neighborhood
of alleys.
Here you slide
and here you
sink, wet, in.
Help me
to indicate
which way
it is
I'm choosing.
Eventually
tempered
by a nice
hostility.

WAIT FOR ME, SUGAR

A man is crawling and a woman
is on fire. Cloud of heads. Porcupine
of weapons. Somewhere is someone
holding open a book. This is
Judas Kiss. Do not suffer me.

MOTHERHOOD HAS MADE ME HONEST

I am trying to think what Rome
smelled like when I was a child, how people
walking in pairs there seemed to wear
matching shirts.

In some dream I just had
I maniacally performed
weeping. I am most terrified when you shut
the door of your voice.

VALLEY SONG

My will is speckled with lights
and climbing the sinuous
road. One wild pink tree.
Bones of what was built
before, and for miles,
smoke slow like clouds.
A taller guess—birds call
sharp and loud across morning.
As behind a curtain, the bright
greens and browns of day.

Terrace, open like a palm—
for every kindness, an expectation.
The vagueness of haze
is unlike the vagueness of water,
as far as my eye can see.

SERENISSIMA

The cobbled street behind me and its own impossible bridge.
Amphibian night comes on. What I fear is transformation.

They walk through the night as though it isn't closing in on us.
I had meant to catch the slant of dimming light, to keep track

while it fell and then feel reckless. Panic at the fish market.
Panic at the intersection of canal and street. I am more romantic

than they are. And more scared. In my long narrow room,
I keep my head near the heart. This hotel, a wet night that extends.

WOULD YOU LIKE TO SEE MY HOUSE

1.
Our garden, inexplicable.
All day, we watered. We were removed.

All night, a metronomic noise,
like the mattress springs of honeymooners.

2.
Each of us
at dinner

has experimented
with silence.

3.
At night we believe
the sculptures on the lawn are our feelings.

The path is tricky.
There are beacons of rock.

Has there been some other nourishing?

4.
She is painting one wall.
Wed to it, she is red.

THE DREAM IS ABOUT US

Attempted to pilfer the definition of homesickness.
Grass level, gentle slope. To those plagued by guilt,

may there be continuous planning
for the unimaginable. Greater care in the loading

and unloading of hearts. Winter looms.
Its are a practical range of demands. It is beautiful

to imagine inevitability. Dropped, meaning planted.

THE PAMPERED ACTRESS
HAS WITNESSED A MURDER

This is no place for the numinous. Remains
a question of access. What is self-
consciousness and where does she keep it.
Drowned man in a fenced-in pool.
She hits a wave of nostalgia.

MOVING PICTURE

Don't look: An affair is beginning. With height and like a creature he reappears. Woman him down! But there's a wife, his wife. The detective is his own masterpiece when intrigue starts. Once we're in or near the center there's police deceit. Awry. He turns across. Ensnared. A heated run.

THERE ARE THE OBVIOUS THINGS
AND WE WANT THEM

Regarding the dime novel, see penny dreadful. In one
thought experiment all our hopes are made of words.
Sometimes it's sadder to say it's not sad—affections
of the thinking organs suffer less when named. We're
sleeping when they come to get us. Serial hope is serial risk.
I'm thinking every single day, what we might miss, might have
missed.

STUDY FOR THE HOOK-HANDED MAN

Everywhere the sense

as after falling
down stairs.

Our limbs are a sense.

I've siphoned everything
I possibly could

from myself—these drained
pond bottoms

are now complicated fields.

Oh swamp, oh first
step, oh foot before

the next. Rigid

conviction of a place
pitched on a self.

Bridges emerge, but
of dark, uncertain color.

Is this a wish?
A consolation?

A somewhat clear

indictment
in what I've finally seen.

COMMERCE IN DREAMS
IS BUSINESS AS USUAL

The fire was started by lightning last Friday.
I'd give anything for something great

to live up to. There are several paths
to actual and only some require rosy

thinking. Tonight, though, a man-made
constellation. Each game missing

a single piece; what will we make them with?
A fantastic wish, generally regarded

as impossible? I don't want to tell you
how I'm feeling. Sublimate aggressions:

the hardboiled school. We are living briefly
in the ordered world. We match wits with it.

HERE'S ME

in the weather
worrying
                              (Storm still)
A self-conscious
passenger
riding along in the train

I am having
trouble reading
afraid of being insincere

and thinking: looming permanence

Yes we turn to metaphor in loss but
but   (Storm still)

Perhaps it was imposter

ETIQUETTE LESSONS
FOR A RELUCTANT GRANDDAUGHTER
WHO IS HEIR APPARENT TO THE THRONE

I love the slender, green tree in the courtyard,
its branches level like so many planes. There is nothing
pulling on my heartstrings now. All tucked in

I am weightless. What I can teach you
is who to think about when you feel guileless. When I was
thirsty, I followed one path from the list to the face.

Toss from the left hand what you can't bear in the right.
Or, what you lose for a moment's mirth and wonder.
Persevere, little lamb. Only hunger is straight.

NECESSARY PARENTHESES

To box up what living deforms.
You are earnest. You are desperate to please.

Your pink hat and your pink hat vanishing.
Startled, then cloying, then the glint of teeth.

Why the heart? Why beating?
I right myself: my concavity and my chest.

MOVING PICTURE

Her funny hopes, aristocratic. They keep company with the captain—her own and the sea's. Her true wit shines rich beneath her friends' romances. He is persuaded and rakish: Break this Anne with Anne.

SHE THINKS THAT IS
WHICH APPEARS TO BE

A long time? Hardly.
Instinct fails first, and thus, cuts
the knot. The only cure for madness

is forgetfulness,
and in these few years she's seemed
insane all the time.

Reading, moved by a fluctuating I,
she'd go back to the place
but it's been changed.

The head is just an organ for borrowing.

COMPULSORY SONG

Someone is lost upon the water. Low
again, I'm shaping my nails toward something

rounder, shouldering future until it is warmer.
The hateful in expectation is the lonely

in windows. Someone is making a point,
an artist's project. All our furniture

is inexplicably removed.
A moister morning, unexpectedly close and cool.

We have lost some thing enormous—
in the mud, at the mouth of the bay.

THE ANTITHETICAL MEANING OF PRIMAL WORDS
after Sigmund Freud

1.
These are the stages
for diseases of unbecoming

references to strangers in the gardens
of their words.

It's a gift of composition—
truth's zigzag from her worst.
> (The white of a "no," the straight of an unbinding.)

     "Scaffold" is a drifting
         beginning in the night.

2.
Buried in the words, uncanny ghosts are still wandering. The vestige of use is deep
but not still. Everyone at the table knows about uncertainty. But life is beautiful
and dangerous. We member its daggers in the shadows of the structures.

3.
But for an unthinking
night, for that quality

of night. We had been kind
to each other.
         We were wildly kind.

FEELINGS ARE THE NEW IMAGINATION

A sudden gust of wind and what would
fall flies. What brings to bear bears
bringing—it was not grief, the feeling,

although pickled and dark. A sea sits
better wholly lonely. He'd rather be a shark
than a monster truck driver, rather

water than a wall. These are our seldom
appropriate feathers. I see a hat in the air
and it's dancing. I have forgiven everything.

THE DREAM IS ABOUT US

Purple hearse parked by the boarded-
up church. Mornings I watch the street
from below—how the world seems backlit

when it's raining. I spend the day, spend
the radio, walk as if I can fly. Early,
busy, afternoon, alone. There is

rebuke in the color of the sky. Flat wood
slats: plank to stone. What I call by name
is crowding. Blank-begotten plume.

THE SEASONS WERE ERASING THE YEARS AGAIN

I had been "girl
at the window of the green
hotel." Have mercy.

Have this whole
white bed. There had been
nothing

in sight for miles.
Sand hills were like spines
of a country. We walked

the steep
road to church and then we walked
back down.

Mother of the waters, take
this red heart
and sink it. This island.

His translucent brow.
A donkey on the beach
hefts his deep, straw saddlebags.

(STATION 1)

What joins us in our bags
is a danger I
believed we had sur-
mounted

crying
in Vienna over
schnitzel
after Munich

turning twenty on the top
bunk of a Rome-
bound train

To do dim
homage
to the rain-
speckled window

I condemn them
like a criminal
on her way to exaltation
The divinely ordinary

The particular

shoe I carried
a head for Halloween
bearded belated
more husband

than Holofernes
blood
painstaking paint
Sorry fantasy

my abulia

I COMPROMISE MY SELF

after Luigi Pirandello

1. My Wife and My Nose

Both pending.
Both slightly to the left.

2. Following the Stranger

A number of times, leaving the station, I noticed someone
else leaving, too. I have to decide: Are you plausible? All
 movements are suspicious. I marry my eyes to the glass.

3. Uncomfortable Vicar

Among
the similarly
obsessed.

4. Marco-of-God and his Wife, Diamond

The judge needs time. He is also the doctor.
Someone has been working for weeks.
She read old books in Florence.
She lived there for a long time.

5. Complications

This thing
is total.

6. Green Wool Blanket

I am surprised to see
all of that touching
still going on.

Remind me
how to be comfortable
constantly
in my clothes.

BRIGHTLY LIT AGAINST THIS

The infection in a name will move through a paragraph
from instance to instance of iteration. Really she's a rather
rabid girl. But she borders on sleepiness. She passes on over to sleep.
She is furiously clinging to the germ of her self, kernel
of her matter. Almost completely deprived of words.
Condenses even resistance itself.

MOVING PICTURE

Our heroine loves an uncultured boy, lovely. Their mad young version presents a doomed mad thrust. And all the while this Olivia is sweeping the century's etiquette: married and revealed. Aristocratic family trouble triumphs over patriotism. Is there love after Frederick? Now she's but our window, just a random girl.

WHAT PROPELS TRANSFORMS

I wanted to tell her
the difference between possible
and sustained. Cocoon,
cocoon! Objective
correlative for all the dicey

stops.
It's easy, this assignment,
making forms from resources
available. Just figure
out what's enough and wear it out.

Every time, surprised and salted, an ache
is fretted with natural light.

CONCERNING THE PRIME AND PROPER
FOUNDATION OF BLAME

By mind, the trick of the balm is overridden
        (I used to see myself in the metaphor).

Little person, you'll never be the newest one you know. Another
        morning. Another morning.
                Another morning.

Monochromatic searching for a monochromatic soul.

I've always known how to float. I've just known.
Now to figure out the science
                in the interest of control.

A list of the risks taken:
the sooner, the quicker.

And all the while, nothing knew.

BATHING THE BABY

Inspect her mouth but do not injure the tender
membranes. This is a new

way of seeing.
She stalks so quietly.

You think I am less
decisive than I used to be but I can't decide if that's true.

Like this morning: I insulted
all the poems by everybody. Tuck

her little face, towel under chin.
You may not realize.

A WOMAN REMOVES HER DENTURES
AND GIVES THEM TO HER HUSBAND

I was not always

this way
I mean I'd give you
anything

My belly still rises
behind my ribs

Or it doesn't
I can handle

anything

Ever
harsher judge
of success
        I am made
to forget

MOVING PICTURE

Among the can't, he is smitten with her talents, dirt-poor, in this most enigmatic film. A factory plagued, his hardscrabble Alice. Naïve man, apprentice of arrival, his fantasy of disparate threads is obliterated by survival. A new, witty, popular and dangerous call: In bordello he realizes an "equilibrium." Forgot himself but for his transformation (that captivating demon). If not for the tragedy, he draws supremely, a roughly lined portrait, women physical around.

FALSE PROFUNDITY IN CONFLICT

Other walls in our life are humming
their beautiful squeeze.

It bothers us, mostly, at the
suggestion of others—the reflection of a lamp

in a room that becomes a moon
on someone's portrait.

Your manifesto?

In daylight, we hunt for the hatches

but we aren't trying
to move on. There would be a place?

To stay? If we needed to?

Come hither, my friend,
come in.

AND A TABLE THAT GOES ON FOR MILES

The women's legs look better every year.
His basement, still strung with noosed

ham thighs. There is a cemetery
of stacked boxes and he has loved

it for its photographs. Above his arched
valley, there is the stench of burning

fields. Who built these kennels? And who
is this lovely one insisting: Water runs now.

We have husbands. We don't need you. As though
he could wake and believe that his country was real.

THE DREAM IS ABOUT US

The sea swallows bodies
and spits them out smarter.

Sob of your iron
on the black linen dress.

At crosswalks startled
by the proximity of strangers,

faces at windows.
The wave of you comes and comes.

What a strange thing a house is
when it's not lit up.

SATURDAY, AND GETTING COLDER

Which dark trophies can we relegate to past?

I want feelings that are buildings
and not signs. You tell me:

No one away is coming home.
Not tonight.

So then let's get on our bicycles and ride
in the dark. In absence. In educated guess.

All my new estimates are proving to be right:
A life is as assembled out of thin

birch branches. Now you know
everything: I was unnaturally lit from within.

There,
that's my handbag at the scene of the crime.

Do not "look to me." I will not be prepared.

A WHOLE THINKING NIGHT

out pulling our thoughts—
faint glowing like stars
when the oars slice through.

Feeling warmth about the difference
in a day. Able: you. But if
retracted? A boat still far, but going fast.

Huddled figures bring the night
up close. I was on and good
there, warmth with me still.

Oh emotions, vast and randomized.
Most of all, that
which is not observed.

MOVING PICTURE

Straining for signs and not-so-satisfied, she's out and stalking realism. Telling follows clean drama, and life shifts its preventative gestures. On screen she struggles with knowledge and smiles completely. She is giving her money, all of it, away. Each object suggests a symbol and then it undoes her. The sun, when it is out, is always tragically high.

PEREGRINE

1.
Who will believe you discernible
from the rooms you inhabit?

Eager, complicit,
you aren't dangerous yourself.

Take me to the end
of what you know of me,

knuckles loose
on the wheel.

2.
We have a pack of spoons left.
Both of us have failed.

The smell of self and self,
is it stifling?

First corner. Side of my house.
I know you thought I was lost.

I say wink, but never wanderer.
What we know is aperture.

A THIRD PARTY WHO SAYS ME
after Gilles Deleuze

City is a way of forgetting
the darkness that surrounds us

so fly me east toward the gathering
of names.

It's a dance of mechanics,
just a couple of lights:

not only, but it's me and lonely.
Sometimes.

In all ugly rooms
all the people are sad.

City is undoing the always
that performs us:

Here I am!
In this space between the lights,

making the space greater
pushing the lines apart.

This is for someone who has forgotten
her flight.

Silly to think we had to know
each other's mind

I mean
how dare you.

There isn't meaning in what we say.
Improvise a little,

just a couple of lines.
We move each other
around.

I SLEEP IN MY BED WITH NO FLOOR TO LAND ON

Landed in Kansas City among bare trees
and America—what seems to be open might
soon be closed. This is the way

the unimaginable happens: Imagined nemesis,
I am easily tricked. Now the dense grids

of buildings are like textured fields,
and we cruise above a glancing city.
Only touch the ground to know how fast

we've been flying. In the direction of travel
I would make a left. Steal time—take time.

Have time—make time. Terminal One.
What seems to be open might soon be closed:
the same thing with the other words.

QUESTION AS ARTICULATED LONGING

Into words, into woods, every
strike is acoustic.
How to say something

open and awful, now,
with the music of the parade
all around us. We did the unthinkable:

closed the windows
against night. Not wishing
to be part of those things which I am
part of this is just feeling sorry.

I'd like to be working on a context
as well
as marvelous disguises.

Always a dark would. We might
make our way through,
might call something,

wonder how its parts interact.
This is what it feels like.

A CORPSE TELLS HOW SHE DIED
AND WHO WAS INVOLVED IN HER DEATH

You've done a study of the woman in the downtown window.
Blow dries her hair, smokes cigarette after cigarette. Everything is falling.

Nothing is lost. I keep a small bronze bust of the fortune-teller's namesake
and I have sized up my opponents. They were all carrying knives.

Nod, though you're not quite sure. Everything I have you have
seen and heard. Of all, after all, we were lost lost lost.

MOVING PICTURE

Murdered honeymoon, a burglary gone bad. Cora: embroiled, unraveled, dead. Was an inside woman on her way to blue awry: famished but forgivable. Soon famed gumshoe checks arrivals in the diminutive town. A host under suspicion, open-and-shut. Unspin another everything, there'll be poison for these crimes. Only later we'll be armed.

A DREAM SO RISKY I WANT
TO BE SAVED IN THE MORNING

1.

A child had a vision of a five-headed crane. Nothing
more fierce than his folding. As strong wind
makes us faster than usual. Instantaneous conclusions
upon first touch. Examining my soul
for some sign of election. Press the word,
its physical plant.

2.

When is the defeated landscape oracular? "Poet"
is an idea by which she is not moved. In the other world
I am filled with something other; I open the window
to throw something out. Should we check, together,
what time it is tomorrow? We all will have moved
there from home.

AGAINST SHIPWRECK

We are cocked, about
to circle each other

indefinitely. A sound,
not unlike the thrum

of sustained thunder.
It isn't here you wait,

it's around the bend.
Oh the motions. Fumble

in the pocket for some
necessary stay. I want to

make big things fly.
Make them fall and break

irrevocably. Start seaward.
Make "marry" weigh.

RADIO SILENCE

What is the position in which we're tumbling from
the ship? To make a wake, or what's behind us,
I take the words I like. A voice that thrills, a killing.
Let's look up the currents where there are people
we know. There is much in this system, every
other plunge. In another dark scene the shore's
receding. A shape our voices make is "ought."

THE DREAM IS ABOUT US

All quiets in this season-long
half-light. All morning I have followed
the briefest of sun shafts. We are sad

and so we can identify the weight
and shape of our hearts. I am shot
to death. This is how it begins.

Posit me, engaged as I am in constant
miscommunication. I've visited a place
with a different cyclical climate. Here,

this strange pink sky persists—
it is seething. At the end of the block is a tunnel
that will take us to Italy. Already

they are stringing the lanterns along the cliff.

photo by Youngsuk Suh

Stefania Heim holds an M.F.A. in Poetry from Columbia University and is completing a Ph.D. in English at the CUNY Graduate Center, writing a dissertation called *Dark Matter: Susan Howe, Muriel Rukeyser, and the Scholar's Art.* Her various writings— poems, essays, and translations—have appeared in *A Public Space, Aufgabe, Jacket2, The Journal of Narrative Theory, The Literary Review, The Paris Review,* and elsewhere. She is a founding editor of *CIRCUMFERENCE: Poetry in Translation* and in 2014 will become a poetry editor at *The Boston Review.* She has taught at Columbia University, Deep Springs College, and Hunter College. She was raised in Queens, NY.

NOTES

The poems in the "Moving Pictures" series reference, mix, and explore plots, images, and characters from a range of films and texts, including *I Vitelloni*, *Nights of Cabiria*, *The Postman Always Rings Twice*, and *Persuasion*.

The titles "The Pampered Actress Has Witnessed a Murder" and "Etiquette Lessons for a Reluctant Granddaughter Who Is Heir Apparent to the Throne" are taken from lines in Brett Fletcher Lauer's poem "Adult Situations."

"Study for the Hook-Handed Man" borrows imagery from Susan Howe's essay "Incloser" in *The Birth-mark: unsettling the wilderness in American literary history*.

The refrain "(Storm still)" in "Here's Me" is taken from the repeated stage direction in Act III of Shakespeare's *King Lear*.

The title and last line of "She Thinks That Is Which Appears To Be" are riffs on Thoreau's lines in *Walden*: "We think that that is which appears to be" and "My instinct tells me that my head is an organ for burrowing."

"The Antithetical Meaning of Primal Words" began as a homophonic translation of Sigmund Freud's essay of the same name (with thanks to Wayne Koestenbaum for the assignment).

"Feelings Are the New Imagination" is inspired, in part, by Jeff Wall's photograph, "A Sudden Gust of Wind (after Hokusai)."

"I Compromise Myself" uses language, characters, and ideas loosely translated from Luigi Pirandello's novel, *Uno, nessuno e centomila*.

The title "Concerning the Prime and Proper Foundation of Blame" is taken from Jonathan Edwards' "The Mind."

The titles "False Profundity in Conflict" and "A Third Party Who Says Me" are taken from Gilles Deleuze's *Difference and Repetition*.

"Question as Articulated Longing" is indebted to lectures by Joan Richardson. The line "Every strike is acoustic" references Joseph Beuys' remark that "every mark you put on paper is acoustic," as echoed and cited by Susan Howe.